Original title:
The Things We Leave

Copyright © 2024 Swan Charm
All rights reserved.

Author: Sabrina Sarvik
ISBN HARDBACK: 978-9916-89-772-0
ISBN PAPERBACK: 978-9916-89-773-7
ISBN EBOOK: 978-9916-89-774-4

The Solace of Timeless Remnants

In the quiet of the night, we find,
Echoes of the past that bind.
Wisdom flows from ages gone,
In shadows cast, spirits drawn.

Beneath the stars, we seek to feel,
The tender touch of grace so real.
In every whisper, love resides,
A guiding light that never hides.

Memories woven, a sacred thread,
In every heart, the verses spread.
Time's embrace, a gentle hand,
Leading us to the promised land.

From the ashes, hope will rise,
Awakening dreams beneath the skies.
For in each moment, truth remains,
In timeless remnants, love sustains.

God Whispered in Empty Spaces

In silence thick, where shadows play,
God's voice can gently sway.
Through the void, His spirit calls,
In empty spaces, love enthralls.

A breeze that stirs the barren air,
Divine intention fills the spare.
Hearts attuned to sacred signs,
In the stillness, He defines.

Every tear that falls in grace,
Is caught and cherished in His embrace.
In desolation, hope ignites,
A beacon bright through endless nights.

With every heartbeat, whispers grow,
In quietude, the spirit flows.
In the emptiness, a hymn we sing,
For God speaks softly in everything.

When Shadows Carry Our Secrets

In twilight's hush, our secrets dwell,
Shadows dance, and stories tell.
Whispers float on twilight's breeze,
In hidden corners, hearts appease.

Each shadow holds a tender truth,
A fragment of our fleeting youth.
Bearing burdens, silent stress,
In shadows' arms, we find redress.

For in the dark, a light can gleam,
Reflecting every hidden dream.
Through shadows thick, compassion flows,
In their embrace, the spirit grows.

We share our fears with paths unseen,
In mutual trust, we glean.
Within the shadows, we unite,
Holding secrets, finding light.

The Divine Canvas of Absence

Upon the canvas, absence speaks,
A silent prayer in longing peaks.
Every stroke a heart laid bare,
In absence, love's bright threads ensnare.

The empty spaces, wide and vast,
Remind us of the heart's steadfast.
In every void, a promise waits,
A sacred bond that transcends fates.

Through tears of loss, we learn to see,
The beauty found in memory.
For absence paints a rich design,
In every moment, the divine.

The echoes linger, soft and clear,
A testament to those held dear.
In the absence, grace abides,
The divine canvas forever rides.

Divinely Disposed Memories

In quiet prayer, whispers of the past,
Echoes of love, a bond that will last.
Hearts entwined in faith's gentle embrace,
Cherished moments time cannot erase.

Each tear we've shed, a lesson learned well,
In grace, we rise, through trials we dwell.
The light of hope, forever it glows,
In the garden of love, our spirit grows.

Traces of Grace in Shadows

In the twilight, shadows softly sweep,
Footprints of grace, in silence they keep.
Guiding our hearts through the dark of night,
Illuminated paths, the soul's pure light.

Each moment beckons, a divine call,
In humble whispers, we rise or fall.
May we find strength in the depths of woe,
For grace through shadows helps love to grow.

The Sacrament of Farewell

With heavy hearts, we gather to part,
Anointed memories, stitched to the heart.
In sacred silence, we share our pleas,
Holding on tightly, like leaves on the breeze.

Faith guides the way as we bid adieu,
In every farewell, we find something new.
The bonds of love, though stretched far and wide,
In the sacred sacrament, we abide.

Heavenly Hues of Separation

As dawn breaks softly, a new day begins,
Colors of heaven, where love never thins.
Though miles may stretch, our spirits will fly,
In vibrant hues, our connections don't die.

Each sunset whispers, a gentle goodbye,
Yet hope remains, as we reach for the sky.
In the tapestry woven with love from above,
Separation's beauty is painted in love.

Echoes of Abandonment

In shadows deep where silence dwells,
The heart recalls its whispered spells.
Each prayer unfurls like dying leaves,
A testament to what deceives.

Once vibrant voices fade away,
Lost melodies in disarray.
Yet in the stillness, echoes remain,
Of love now wrapped in gentle pain.

The sky, a canvas brushed with gray,
Reflects the dreams that went astray.
Hope's flicker dims but does not die,
In sorrow's grip, we still will try.

From ashes rise the hearts of yore,
Carried forth on winds that soar.
Abandoned paths now line the soul,
In sacred search for one true goal.

Remnants of Forgotten Faith

Where once we stood with spirits high,
Now dust lays thick, and shadows sigh.
The stones of altars, worn and bare,
Whisper stories lost in prayer.

Time's gentle hand has smoothed the stone,
But faith remains, not quite alone.
In hearts that ache, a flicker glows,
The remnants of what love once chose.

The pages torn from ancient books,
Speak of longing in downcast looks.
Yet every tear a comment makes,
On echoes soft that never break.

In twilight's grasp, we gently tread,
Through hallowed halls where dreams once spread.
What we have lost, we cannot claim,
Yet in the stillness, love's the same.

Silent Whispers of Departed Souls

Beneath the moon, where shadows creep,
The whispers of the lost still seep.
In every breeze, their voices call,
A haunting song within us all.

They wander far on paths unseen,
In quiet realms, where hearts convene.
Each flickering light, a guiding star,
Reminds us who they truly are.

In every tear, a story weaves,
Of love and loss, what one believes.
Though time may take them far from sight,
Their presence lingers, pure and bright.

With every prayer, they hear our plea,
As silent guardians, they are free.
In sacred moments, souls unite,
In shadows deep, they share their light.

The Altar of Lost Moments

Atop the hill, where spirits roam,
Lies an altar, stripped of home.
Each moment spent, a sacred vow,
Now rests in time's relentless flow.

The past is etched in every stone,
A collection of the heart's own throne.
Where laughter reigned, now silence falls,
As memory in twilight calls.

Yet beauty blooms in whispered grace,
In every loss, a soft embrace.
For moments lost are never vain,
In love's remembrance, we'll remain.

We gather round this sacred site,
In search of peace, we find the light.
Though time has turned what once was bright,
The altar holds our hopes in sight.

The Blessing of Letting Go

In the silence of the night, we find,
The weight of burdens left behind.
With open hands, we release the past,
Embracing freedom that comes at last.

In faith, we trust the greater plan,
Surrendering dreams into His hands.
Each tear that falls, a seed of grace,
In the garden of His loving embrace.

For every loss, a lesson blooms,
In the shadows, light still looms.
With every breath, we learn to see,
The beauty in our own decree.

From ashes rise new paths to tread,
In the stillness, the Spirit led.
Letting go, we learn to grow,
In His mercy's gentle flow.

A newfound dance, a sacred song,
In surrender, we feel we belong.
With every step, He guides our way,
In the blessing of a brand new day.

Eternal Footprints in Time

In sands of time, our stories blend,
With whispers soft, the heavens send.
Footprints laid through ages past,
In every moment, shadows cast.

Each step we take, a mark defined,
In love's embrace, our souls entwined.
The echoes of our laughter ring,
In memories, a sacred thing.

Through trials faced, we rise above,
In every heart, a spark of love.
The footprints left, a map divine,
In every life, a sacred sign.

As stars align in night's embrace,
We find our strength in endless grace.
In gratitude, we walk this land,
With hope and dreams, forever planned.

In twilight's glow, the journey streams,
In every breath, our story gleams.
Eternal footprints, side by side,
In timeless grace, we shall abide.

Sacred Dust of Vulnerable Moments

In shadows cast by trembling hands,
We gather hope where silence stands.
Each fragile breath, a whispered prayer,
Embraced by light, suspended air.

In fleeting time, our spirits dance,
In every fall, we find romance.
The sacred dust, it weaves our dreams,
Through fragile threads, the heart redeems.

When silence falls on weary souls,
In gentle folds, the story rolls.
The vulnerable meet divine embrace,
In moments soft, we find our place.

As dawn arrives, the shadows fade,
We rise anew, our fears betrayed.
With every step, we seek the light,
In sacred dust, we find our flight.

Within this space, our hearts align,
In trust and grace, we intertwine.
Through fragile moments, we ascend,
To sacred dust, our souls transcend.

Litanies of the Unremembered

In whispered prayers, the echoes call,
For souls forgotten, who gave their all.
We sing of love that time erased,
In litanies, their names embraced.

In shadows cast by fleeting years,
We honor lives, shrouded in tears.
Each name a prayer, a heart reclaimed,
In the book of life, forever named.

For every voice that fades away,
Their stories woven, night to day.
Through hurt and hope, we seek the grace,
In remembering, we find our place.

The silence deep, yet love surrounds,
In sacred spaces, their truth resounds.
With every breath, their spirits rise,
A symphony beneath the skies.

In gratitude, we carry forth,
The light they brought, a gentle north.
Unseen yet felt, a legacy,
In our hearts, they still wander free.

The Path We Walked Unseen

In the quiet, footsteps trace,
A journey shared, though not a race.
Through valleys dark and mountains high,
In faith we wander, hand in sky.

The shadows dance, the light will blend,
In sacred moments, time will mend.
Each step a story, each breath a prayer,
The path we walked, though rarely bare.

With every stumble, lessons bloom,
In the garden of our hearts' own room.
Together forged in trials great,
The ties of love will not abate.

In silence shared, our spirits soar,
Through unmarked ways, we seek for more.
The unseen bond, a guiding light,
In unity, we find our might.

As seasons shift and days unfold,
In every tale, a truth retold.
With open hearts, we boldly stride,
The path we walked, with faith our guide.

The Blessing of What Remains Unspoken

In honor of the things unsaid,
The prayers that linger, words that bled.
A stillness grows where hearts can dwell,
In quiet realms, we weave our spell.

Each glance, a promise wrapped in grace,
The silence holds a sacred space.
In muted tones, our truths await,
The blessing lies in love's innate.

Within the hush, we find our song,
In soft confessions, we belong.
What remains unspoken, treasured, dear,
The whispers linger, ever near.

The beauty found in every sigh,
In wordless bonds, we learn to fly.
Through silent vows, we gain our voice,
In unexpressed, we make our choice.

Together in the stillness born,
A dance of souls, in twilight's morn.
The blessing rests where hearts can see,
In what remains, we are set free.

Fragments of Faith in Every Farewell

In every parting, grace takes flight,
The heart remembers, holds on tight.
Fragments of faith, like scattered stars,
Illuminate paths, no matter how far.

Each goodbye breathes a sacred trust,
In whispered vows, our bond is just.
Faith lights the way through stormy seas,
In every farewell, a soft breeze.

Through tears we gather, strength anew,
In loss, we find the love so true.
In every farewell, a journey's end,
Yet faith remains, our eternal friend.

The echoes fade, yet memories gleam,
A tapestry woven of faith's dream.
In every farewell, we find our call,
To rise again, to never fall.

In fragments held, our spirits soar,
Through faith's embrace, we are restored.
Every goodbye, a seed that's sown,
In sacred hearts, we are not alone.

The Hushed Psalm of Lost Possessions

In gentle whispers, loss unfolds,
The tales of treasures, yet untold.
A hymn of what the heart has bared,
In hushed psalms, our souls are shared.

Each item lost, a fleeting sign,
A memory wrapped in love's design.
The echoes linger in empty space,
In every loss, we find our grace.

From ashes rise the things we keep,
In tender moments, we learn to weep.
The beauty found in every scar,
In lost possessions, we reach afar.

Through silent prayers, we let them go,
In loss, we find what hearts can sow.
Hushed psalms echo in twilight's glow,
In every tear, the love will flow.

In gratitude, we bless the pain,
In all we've lost, our spirits gain.
The psalm we sing, a sacred trust,
In every loss, love's path is just.

The Stillness of Unspoken Grief

In silence, hearts do mourn and bend,
The weight of loss, a sacred friend.
In whispered prayers, the tears do flow,
A gentle light in sorrow's glow.

Each memory, a cherished spark,
In shadows deep, we feel the dark.
Yet hope resides, though dimmed it seems,
In faith and love, we find our dreams.

Through aching nights, the spirit stirs,
In wounds that speak without their blurs.
With every breath, a story told,
In grief, the heart learns to be bold.

The dawn will rise, though night is long,
In softest notes, we'll sing a song.
For even in the deepest pain,
Resilience blooms – a sweet refrain.

So linger not in sorrow's chains,
For in the stillness, love remains.
Embrace the grief, but rise above,
In every loss, there's hidden love.

Glimmers of Light in Shadowed Paths

In twilight's grasp, where shadows creep,
A flicker shines, it's ours to keep.
The weary traveler finds their way,
With guiding stars in skies of gray.

Through tangled woods and burdens borne,
A lantern glows, the heart reborn.
Each step we take, though fraught with fear,
Reveals the light that's always near.

With every trial, a lesson learned,
In darkest times, our spirits yearned.
For hope is forged in persevered faith,
And from the struggle, we find our wraith.

So walk with grace, O weary soul,
With every stumble, closer to whole.
The road ahead may twist and wind,
But seek, and solace you will find.

In laughter's echo, in sorrow's song,
The light will lead your heart along.
For in the shadowed paths we roam,
Glimmers of grace will guide us home.

Echoed Blessings in Empty Rooms

In corners where the silence dwells,
The whispered prayers, a soft repels.
Against the walls, the memories cling,
In empty rooms, the heart takes wing.

Each breath we draw, an echo sweet,
In empty spaces, love repeats.
With every shadow that softly falls,
A chorus of the heart recalls.

The laughter shared, the tears we shed,
In this still haven, we're not misled.
For sacred bonds, though unseen they be,
Resound in warmth, eternally free.

In gentle light, the past unfurls,
In every moment, the blessing swirls.
In quietude, we find our grace,
In empty rooms, we find our place.

So honor all that came before,
In echoes soft, our spirits soar.
For what was lost shall ever loom,
In the beauty of these empty rooms.

The Unseen Ties of Yesterday

In threads of time, our lives entwined,
The unseen ties that love defined.
With every glance, a story spun,
In yesterday's embrace, we run.

Through laughter shared and sorrow's weight,
The bonds we forge, a timeless fate.
In every heartbeat, echoes call,
In quiet moments, we are all.

For in the past, our roots run deep,
In whispered memories, secrets keep.
Though seasons change, and time may fly,
The heart recalls, and soars the sky.

With hands held high, we face the dawn,
In gratitude for all that's gone.
For unseen ties, like threads of light,
Will guide us through the dark of night.

So cherish well each shared refrain,
In yesterday's love, there's no disdain.
For in those ties, our souls connect,
In every moment, we reflect.

Lanterns of Memory Guiding Us

In the stillness of the night,
Lanterns flicker soft and light.
Carried by the winds of grace,
Guiding hearts to sacred space.

Whispers of the past resound,
In every corner, love is found.
Beneath the stars, we seek our way,
With memories that softly sway.

Through valleys deep, our souls do roam,
In every heart, we find a home.
The lanterns shine, a beacon clear,
Illuminating paths we hold dear.

Hope rekindles in the dark,
As each flame ignites a spark.
Together we journey, hand in hand,
Lanterns of memory, a holy band.

Let not the shadows steal our light,
For faith will carry us through night.
With every step, we draw anew,
The warmth of love that guides us true.

The Altar of Forgotten Journeys

Upon the altar, time once bled,
With dreams and hopes, where paths were tread.
A tapestry of grace unfolds,
As tales of old are gently told.

Here lie the echoes of our past,
Moments lived that forever last.
In silent prayer, we lift our voice,
To honor dreams, to make the choice.

Forgotten journeys, we recall,
In whispers soft, we heed the call.
With every tear, a lesson learned,
In faith, our hearts, they brightly burned.

As we gather 'round the flame,
Each flicker holds a sacred name.
We honor love that guides us still,
In memories deep, our spirits fill.

The altar stands, a testament,
To every soul's devoted bent.
From shadows cast, new light shall spring,
In unity, our hearts will sing.

The Quiet Lament of Time

In the hush of twilight's glow,
Time whispers secrets we must know.
Silent tears upon the page,
We mark the seasons, turn the stage.

Each moment lost, a fragile sigh,
Like driftwood floating, passing by.
A quiet lament fills the air,
For dreams that linger, hope laid bare.

Through the corridors of the past,
We search for treasures meant to last.
In the stillness, pain finds peace,
And in acceptance, shadows cease.

Time, a river, strong and wide,
Carries us forth, our hearts collide.
Yet in the quiet, we still find,
A tapestry of love entwined.

Let not sorrow steal our breath,
For in each ending, life bequeaths.
A promise gleams, in fading light,
The quiet lament, a path to bright.

Echoes of the Divine in Our Absence

In the silence of our parting,
Echoes linger, softly starting.
A gentle touch, a whispered prayer,
Reminds us love is always there.

In absence felt, the spirit flies,
Through every tear, our heart complies.
Divine reflections in the night,
Guide us onward, toward the light.

We gather strength from memories shared,
In every heart, a love declared.
Though space may stretch, our souls embrace,
In unity, we find our place.

Through shadows cast, the dawn shall rise,
With every breath, we realize.
The divine is woven in our fate,
In absence, we celebrate.

Together still, though far apart,
The echoes of love fill every heart.
A melody sweet, from heavens above,
In absence found, unending love.

Remnants of Faith Beneath the Stars

In twilight's glow, we seek the light,
Faint whispers of truth, in the quiet night.
Stars above, like spirits, shine,
Holding secrets divine, so very fine.

Each heartbeat echoes, a prayer untold,
In the silence of space, our hopes unfold.
Beneath these heavens, we find our way,
Guided by love, not led astray.

Miracles linger in the shadows cast,
Each memory cherished, forever to last.
Though time may fade, faith will remain,
In the remnants of love, there's no pain.

Hearts united, as we journey on,
In the tapestry woven, faith is strong.
Together we rise, as spirits soar,
In the embrace of night, forevermore.

The Tears We Shed in Sacred Goodbye

In echoes of love, we gather near,
With heavy hearts, we shed our tear.
Each drop a memory, a moment shared,
In the sacred circle, we show we cared.

Parting ways in the dimming light,
As shadows dance, we prepare for flight.
Beneath the weight of our blessed sorrow,
We find the strength for a new tomorrow.

In the heart's embrace, we hold on tight,
To the promises made in the soft twilight.
Though distance may part us, we still remain,
In the fabric of love, there's no disdain.

Each tear a testament, a loving call,
In the aftermath, we rise from the fall.
For in goodbye, there's love embraced,
A holy whisper that can't be erased.

Fragments of Prayer in Departured Souls

In the quiet dusk, we gather our thoughts,
For those who departed, we feel the knots.
Each fragment of prayer released to the skies,
Echoes of voices, that never say goodbyes.

With every flicker, a candle ignites,
A beacon of hope, through the darkest nights.
In whispers of longing, their spirits awake,
In the sacred silence, our hearts do quake.

Through laughter and tears, their journey told,
In the tapestry woven, their stories unfold.
As we gather in faith, our spirits entwine,
The essence of love will always combine.

For those we have lost, we carry the flame,
In the dance of the stars, we say their name.
Between each breath, we find serenity,
In the fragments of prayer, there's unity.

Celestial Elegy of Our Farewells

In celestial echoes, we bid adieu,
To the souls that we cherish, forever true.
With every farewell, a promise remains,
In the sunlight's glow, love never wanes.

As constellations guide our wandering hearts,
In the harmony of life, we play our parts.
Through night's gentle whisper, we share our grief,
In the dance of remembrance, we find relief.

With every heartbeat, their essence resides,
In the shadows of moments, where love abides.
We gather in silence, as tears fall like rain,
In the elegy sung, they live once again.

For each goodbye is a step to the light,
In the arms of the heavens, everything feels right.
Through the cosmic weave, we find our grace,
In the celestial love, there's always a place.

Divine Ripples from the Past

In shadows cast by ancient light,
Whispers echo through the night,
Lessons learned and stories spun,
In the glow, we become one.

Faithful hearts, our spirits soar,
Guided by the tales of yore,
From the depths of sacred streams,
We awaken in our dreams.

Each moment sings a hallowed tune,
Beneath the watchful eye of moon,
In the stillness, wisdom flows,
Through the ages, love bestows.

We gather 'round the fire bright,
Sharing glimpses of the light,
Hand in hand, we seek the truth,
In the heart of ageless youth.

As we tread on sacred ground,
In this space, the lost are found,
With open arms, the past awaits,
In divine ripples, love creates.

The Hallowed Ground of Memory

In the garden where we tread,
Sow the seeds of what is said,
In each thought, a sacred flame,
Hallowed ground calls out our name.

Whispers linger in the air,
Every moment, every prayer,
Through the corridors of time,
Memory sings an ancient rhyme.

With golden light, the past unfolds,
In the silence, truth beholds,
Each heartbeat echoes joy and pain,
In remembrance, love remains.

Gather here, beneath the sky,
In unity, we learn to fly,
Hands entwined, we break the chain,
In the hallowed, we sustain.

From the depths, our spirits rise,
Like the stars that grace the skies,
In this space, our souls ignite,
The hallowed ground glows ever bright.

In the Quiet We Are Known

In the quiet, hearts align,
Silence speaks, both pure and fine,
In the stillness, truths are shared,
In this moment, we are bared.

Cloaked in whispers, souls connect,
In the void, we learn to reflect,
Words unspoken weave a thread,
In the quiet, love is fed.

Gentle thoughts like river streams,
Flow through us, as light redeems,
In the calm, our spirits grow,
Through the peace, we come to know.

As the shadows softly sway,
Guided by the light of day,
In the quiet, we find grace,
Every heartbeat, a warm embrace.

In the stillness, hope takes flight,
Carried forth by sacred light,
In the quiet, we are shown,
That in love, we are not alone.

In Silent Farewell We Find Grace

In stillness we gather our hearts,
Holding the breath of the past,
With whispered prayers, we embark,
Into the night, shadows cast.

Each tear that falls like gentle rain,
Cleanses the wounds we cannot see,
In silence, we cherish the pain,
Embracing the love left to be.

The echoes of laughter now fade,
Yet in the silence, we know,
That every moment we've laid,
Is woven into the soul's flow.

As dawn breaks with tender light,
We seek the grace found in farewells,
In every sorrow, in every fight,
A love everlasting dwells.

In silent farewells, we receive,
The gifts of those who have gone,
In memories sweet, we believe,
Their spirit lingers on and on.

Echoes of Memories at Twilight

At twilight's glow, we meet again,
Where memories softly blend,
In the hushed embrace of the night,
Whispers of love that never end.

The stars adorn the velvet sky,
Each one a tale of yesteryear,
In the silence, we hear their sigh,
An echo of laughter, a tear.

With every shadow that dances near,
The past becomes a guiding light,
In the stillness, we draw them near,
Holding their spirits, warm and bright.

Each moment shared a sacred bond,
A testament to love's pure grace,
In twilight's glow, we are not gone,
For in our hearts, they find a place.

As night falls, our souls intertwine,
With echoes that fill the deep space,
In the silence, we glimpse divine,
In memories' embrace, we find grace.

Sanctuaries of the Departed

Within the heart lie sacred halls,
Where whispers of spirits remain,
Sanctuaries built by soft calls,
Holding the love in their name.

In every corner, a story lives,
Of laughter, of hope, and of tears,
The essence of life truly gives,
Strength to withstand all our fears.

Beneath the stars, we build the space,
Where memories find their true home,
A shelter of love, a warm embrace,
In quiet reflection, we roam.

The departed walk with us still,
In dreams and the calm of the night,
Their presence, a comfort, a thrill,
Guiding our hearts toward the light.

In sanctuaries, peace we sow,
Where time cannot wither or fade,
For every memory helps us grow,
In the love of the life they made.

Shadows of Yesterday's Embrace

In shadows cast by yesterday,
We find the remnants of our past,
Their gentle warmth whispers to stay,
In the heart, their love holds fast.

Each memory like a soft refrain,
Plays in the quiet of the night,
In shadows, we welcome the pain,
Finding solace in love's light.

With every sunset, they draw near,
In twilight's breath, they softly sigh,
Their laughter wraps us, pure and clear,
In shadows, they never say goodbye.

In the depths of our souls, we trace,
The patterns of life intertwined,
In the shadows of love's embrace,
A sacred bond, forever aligned.

Through time and beyond, we remain,
In shadows deep, their spirits rise,
In yesterday's whispers, the pain,
Becomes a bridge to the skies.

The Holy Echo of Farewell

In quiet grace, we gather here,
To bid adieu with hearts sincere.
The whispers of the past remain,
In echoes soft, like gentle rain.

With every tear, a prayer we send,
To those who journey, to the end.
Their spirits rise on wings of light,
As shadows fade into the night.

In sacred moments, time stands still,
A love that lingers, yet to fill.
We hold their memories near and dear,
In every sigh, they still are here.

For in the silence, we shall hear,
The holy echoes, ever clear.
A symphony of soul's refrain,
The bond of love shall not be slain.

So let us lift our hearts in song,
For those who've ventured, brave and strong.
In every farewell, there's a trace,
Of divine grace and warm embrace.

Threads of Devotion in the Light of Leaving

In twilight's glow, we weave our prayers,
With threads of love, our spirit bears.
Each moment shared, a sacred thread,
In light of leaving, memories spread.

With gentle hands, we touch the past,
In devotion, hopes are cast.
We cherish bonds that will not fray,
In every heart, they find their way.

The fabric of our lives entwines,
With colors bright like holy signs.
In every farewell, a promise stays,
A tapestry of timeless ways.

As journeys call, we bid goodbye,
Yet faith will lift our spirits high.
In shadows long, a guiding light,
Threads of devotion shining bright.

Lanterns of Hope in the Dark of Departure

In darkest hours, we hold our flame,
Lanterns of hope, we call their name.
Through shadowed paths, they lead the way,
In every heartbeat, night and day.

With every step, the light will glow,
A beacon bright for those we know.
In parting's grasp, they shall not fade,
For love's refrain shall never trade.

In whispered prayers, we send them forth,
To journeys new, to endless worth.
Lanterns shining, souls alight,
In dark of departure, faith in sight.

Each tender memory guides our quest,
In every trial, we find our rest.
So hand in hand, we brave the night,
With lanterns of hope, our spirits bright.

Heavenly Residue of Cherished Days

In every dawn, a light appears,
Heavenly residue, through tears.
With every smile, a memory wakes,
In cherished days, our spirit breaks.

With gentle winds, the past does call,
A reminder of the love we saw.
In laughter shared, in sorrows too,
The essence of life is ever true.

For in each heartbeat lies a trace,
Of moments caught in time and space.
In holy fragments, love remains,
A tapestry of joys and pains.

So let us gather all we've known,
In heavenly light, we are not alone.
Though days may fade, their glow will stay,
In heavenly residue, we find our way.

The Ocean of What We Never Said

In silence we drift, lost at sea,
Words unspoken, a weight on the soul.
The tides of longing, they pull and plea,
Each wave a whisper, the heart's dark toll.

Beneath the surface, shadows reside,
Cloaked in mystery, they beckon deep.
Promises linger, where dreams coincide,
We navigate paths that the spirit keeps.

Castles of hope built on sandy shore,
Those dreams like shells, washed away with grace.
Yet even in loss, we search for more,
In waters vast, we still find our place.

Held by the currents of fate's own hand,
We seek connection in the depths unknown.
In the ocean of what we never planned,
The heart finds solace, though far from home.

And when the storm rages, light shines through,
A beacon of peace in the falling night.
For in our silence, there lies a true view,
The ocean of love is our guiding light.

Grace in the Gaps of Time

Moments suspended, a breath held tight,
Between each tick, the stillness flows.
In the quiet hours, we find our sight,
Where grace resides and true love grows.

Time bends softly, like a willow's sway,
In those sacred spaces, we learn to dream.
The emptiness blooms in a gentle way,
Each pause a promise, life's hidden scheme.

We dance on the edges of what is real,
In the fragile seconds that often flee.
A sacred touch, a balm to heal,
In the gaps of time, we're truly free.

With every heartbeat, we stitch the seams,
Creating a tapestry, soft and wide.
In the delicate dance of our vibrant dreams,
In grace, we walk with the Lord as guide.

So cherish the moments, both small and grand,
In every silence, let love reside.
For grace is the thread that reforges the hand,
In the gaps of time, let our hearts abide.

The Lament of Forsaken Places

Echoes of laughter lost in despair,
Forsaken places, where shadows dwell.
Memories linger, suspended in air,
The stories carved deep, no one will tell.

Once filled with light, now draped in gray,
These hallowed grounds bear the marks of fate.
In silence they wait, in fading day,
Each corner whispers a love too late.

The ruins speak softly of what has been,
Of dreams once cherished, now swept away.
In the stillness, we feel the unseen,
In each abandoned hall, the heart's dull sway.

Yet in this sorrow, a flicker survives,
A hope that dances in cracks of the stone.
In the quiet, resilience derives,
From all that was lost, we are not alone.

So let us remember these spaces gray,
And honor the lives that shaped their grace.
In the lament of what time took away,
We find our home in this sacred place.

Ephemeral Threads of Existence

Life weaves a tapestry, fragile and bright,
Threads of existence, fleeting and fine.
In the soft glow of the morning light,
We dance on the edges of space and time.

Moments are whispers that drift on the breeze,
Glances exchanged in the blink of an eye.
In the blink, the heart learns to seize,
These ephemeral threads and let them fly.

In laughter and tears, the fabric unfolds,
Each stitch a memory, both bitter and sweet.
As stories are sewn, our journey beholds,
The beauty found in the incomplete.

So cherish the colors that blend in the night,
And bask in the warmth of connections made.
For in every thread, even those of slight,
Lie the secrets of love and the light that won't fade.

Though threads may fray as the years draw near,
And moments may vanish like wisps in the air,
The essence of life lingers ever clear,
In the tapestry woven, our souls laid bare.

Light Through the Cracks of Absence

In shadows deep, where silence grows,
A gentle light through cracks it shows,
Whispers of hope in the empty space,
Guiding the lost to a warm embrace.

In moments dark, faith flickers bright,
A candle's glow dispels the night,
Each crack a story, each beam a prayer,
Illuminating paths beyond despair.

From absence blooms a sacred grace,
In barren fields, our souls we face,
Miracles thrive in the hollowed earth,
In absence found, we discover worth.

The echoes sing of love once near,
In every loss, the heart draws near,
For in the void, God's voice resounds,
In cracks of absence, our faith abounds.

So let the light through shadows pour,
A testament of ever-more,
In each small fracture, the dawn will rise,
As light through cracks ignites the skies.

Hymns to Unseen Farewells

In whispered tones, we say goodbye,
To those who soar in heaven's eye,
Their spirits dance, though we can't see,
In hymns of love, they still roam free.

With every tear, a prayer we weave,
For unseen farewells, we must believe,
In quiet moments, their laughter stays,
Guiding us through our darkest days.

Each absence sings a sacred song,
A melody where hearts belong,
The bonds of love, though stretched apart,
Remain forever in the heart.

In twilight's glow, we feel them near,
Their gentle presence calms our fear,
With every star that lights the night,
We find their souls in the softest light.

So let us lift our voices high,
In joyous hymns, beyond the sky,
For unseen farewells are not the end,
But a journey where love will transcend.

Fragments of a Chosen Path

Along the road where shadows tread,
We wander forth on paths we're led,
Each fragment speaks of trials faced,
In faith, we find our steps embraced.

The choices made, like stones we place,
Construct a journey, a sacred space,
In every twist, we learn to grow,
Caught in the rhythm of ebb and flow.

The light above, our guiding star,
Reminds us of just how far,
With every stumble, grace we find,
In each fragment, love intertwined.

Though roads may fork and dreams may fade,
In the heart of faith, we're unafraid,
For fragments push us toward the whole,
As we navigate the depth of soul.

So walk with courage, take each stride,
Feel the spirit ever beside,
In fragments lost, are lessons keen,
A chosen path where truth is seen.

Prayers for What Remains

In quiet moments, we gather round,
To speak of loss and what we've found,
For every ending, a seed is sown,
In prayers for what remains, love's grown.

With heavy hearts, we lift our voice,
In gratitude, we still rejoice,
For every memory, tender grace,
A light that time cannot erase.

In every tear, a story dwells,
In echoes soft, remembrance swells,
We honor those who walked before,
In prayers woven, forevermore.

Though loved ones gone feel far away,
In our hearts, they choose to stay,
For what remains is not just pain,
But love's sweet whisper in the rain.

So let us cherish what we hold,
In prayers for what remains, be bold,
For in our hearts, their light will shine,
A bond eternal, sacred, divine.

Vestiges of Love's Eternal Light

In the shadows where we dwell,
Whispers of a heart do tell.
Each moment loved, a spark ignites,
Veils lifted, revealing our sights.

With every breath, a prayer unfolds,
In gentle hands, true love enfolds.
Beyond the dusk, the dawn will rise,
Mirroring grace in the skies.

Through trials faced, we hold on tight,
Guided by love's eternal light.
In silence deep, our souls entwined,
A bond unbroken, forever defined.

The echoes of laughter remain,
In memories bright, free from pain.
Each heartbeat sings, a song profound,
In the sacred space, love is found.

So let us wander, you and I,
With faith as vast as the boundless sky.
For every step we take in grace,
Draws us closer in this holy space.

As the stars shine down from above,
We find the vestiges of love.
In every sunset and dawn's glow,
Hearts united, ever aglow.

Miracles in the Space Between

In quiet corners of the heart,
Lies the miracle, a sacred part.
In breaths we take and moments shared,
Heaven whispers, love declared.

Each fleeting glance, a gift divine,
In the space between, our hearts align.
Through tempest tides and tranquil seas,
We find our strength upon our knees.

Unseen forces guide our way,
Transforming night into bright day.
In shadows cast, light breaks through,
Love's endless grace, profound and true.

The miracle lies in every choice,
In shared laughter, in love's voice.
With faith at hand, we journey far,
Illuminated by love's bright star.

And when the world feels cold and stark,
Together we'll ignite a spark.
For in this dance of fate we find,
Miracles await, forever intertwined.

So let us cherish, hold and keep,
The sacred bond that runs so deep.
In the space between, hearts unite,
Creating miracles, love's pure light.

Celestial Remains of Our Journeys

Upon the path where we have tread,
Celestial whispers guide the thread.
In every step, the stars conspire,
Awakening our deepest fire.

With every tear, a lesson learned,
In trials faced, our hearts have burned.
Each joy and sorrow, woven tight,
Crafts the fabric, day and night.

As we ascend to realms above,
Our journeys wrapped in endless love.
In cosmic dance, we intertwine,
Reflecting the divine design.

The remnants of what once was ours,
Shimmer like the distant stars.
In echoes soft, our stories blend,
Each journey shared, we comprehend.

With every twinkle that we see,
A piece of us, in reverie.
As celestial remains shine bright,
We forge our path through endless night.

So let us savor, cherish well,
The tales of love we parallel.
For in each heartbeat, time suspends,
Amid celestial journeys, love transcends.

The Echoing Silence of Lost Souls

In whispered dreams, the silence calls,
Echoes linger through ancient halls.
The souls that wander, seeking grace,
In shadows find their sacred place.

In every sigh, a story's spun,
Of battles lost and victories won.
With hearts perplexed, they search the skies,
Clinging to hope that never dies.

Through veils of time, they softly weep,
For love they lost, for promises deep.
A bond unbroken, though far apart,
In silence, they dwell, a song in the heart.

Yet in the stillness, a light appears,
Wiping away the darkest fears.
With gentle nudges from above,
A reminder of never-ending love.

So let us listen, hear their cries,
In every corner where hope lies.
For in the echoing silence, we see,
The spirits of love, forever free.

Together we rise, hand in hand,
Uniting lost souls in this sacred land.
In echoes that sing, through whispers we roam,
Finding our peace, together at home.

The Quiet Requiem of Our Absences

In shadows where silence softly dwells,
The echoes of love weave gentle spells.
Absent hearts in whispered sighs,
In the stillness, our spirit flies.

Each moment lost in time's embrace,
A lingering touch, an empty space.
Yet hope resides in fading light,
A quiet requiem for the night.

We gather the memories, fragile and sweet,
In the heart's garden, where sorrows meet.
From ashes of absence, we arise,
With faith as our wings, we touch the skies.

In every tear, a universe spins,
Through valleys of loss, our journey begins.
A tapestry woven with threads of grace,
In quiet requiem, we find our place.

Sacred Echoes in Every Goodnight

As the stars blink softly in twilight's glow,
We whisper our prayers, as time moves slow.
In sacred echoes, our souls unite,
In the breathing darkness, we find our light.

Each goodnight a promise, a loving embrace,
Carried on wings of divine grace.
In the quiet chambers of the heart,
We share our dreams, never apart.

With every breath, a tale unfolds,
In the stillness, great mysteries are told.
The moon bears witness to our plight,
In the sacred echoes of every night.

The world's chaos fades, as we seek,
In each gentle verse, a loving peak.
With every lullaby, the spirit takes flight,
In sacred echoes, we dance through the night.

The Weight of Blessing in Our Burdens

In trials we carry, a weight profound,
Yet blessings in shadows, silently found.
Through storms that rage, we learn to stand,
Each burden a lesson, guided by hand.

With every struggle, a strength is born,
In the heart's furnace, a spirit reborn.
The weight of blessing, a sacred thread,
We rise from the ashes, where angels tread.

In moments of doubt, we find our light,
A flickering flame in the darkest night.
Through laughter and tears, our paths intertwine,
In the weight of burdens, true love will shine.

Embrace the heaviness, for it's not in vain,
Each weight we carry, we shall remain.
With grace, we journey through valleys of pain,
The weight of blessing, our sweet refrain.

Celestial Signatures on Empty Spaces

In the canvas of night, where dreams collide,
Celestial signatures, our souls confide.
Stars twinkle gently, like whispers above,
In empty spaces, we find our love.

With each glimmering light, a story unfolds,
Of wanderers seeking, of hearts turned bold.
In the vastness of cosmos, our spirits soar,
Celestial signatures guide us evermore.

In shadows that linger, faith brightly gleams,
The tapestry woven with hope and dreams.
In every heartbeat, a rhythm divine,
Celestial signatures, forever we shine.

Embracing the silence, the wonder we chase,
In the depths of our hearts, we find our place.
Through empty spaces, our spirits ignite,
With celestial signatures, we embrace the night.

Fading Fragments of a Blessed Past

In twilight's hush, we reminisce,
Soft whispers dance, a sacred bliss.
Memories linger, like a prayer,
In holy shadows, we are bare.

Gentle echoes from days of yore,
Hearts in reverence, we explore.
Fragments of joy, like stars align,
In the tapestry of the divine.

Forgotten hymns upon the breeze,
A call to hope, a lamp to seize.
Through fading light, we seek your face,
In every breath, we find your grace.

The past, a church, where spirits soar,
With pillars strong, yet hearts that bore.
In every tear, your love remains,
A sacred bond that never wanes.

So let us hold these treasures dear,
In fading light, your voice we hear.
Blessed fragments, though they may rust,
In faith and love, we place our trust.

Divine Comfort in Abandonment

When shadows fall, we feel the night,
In solitude, we seek the light.
Yet in the depths of quiet despair,
Your presence whispers, always there.

The world may turn, its heart may steep,
Yet in our hearts, your love we keep.
A gentle touch upon our soul,
In every loss, you make us whole.

With every tear, a silent plea,
Your arms, O Lord, embrace the free.
In moments stark, we find your grace,
Divine comfort in this sacred space.

Abandonment, a heavy chain,
But through the pain, we rise again.
In faith's warm hand, our fears subside,
In you, O God, we will abide.

So let us walk this path anew,
With every step, we cling to you.
In the quiet, where hearts unite,
We find our peace in endless light.

Ghostly Heirlooms of Heartfelt Worship

In whispered prayers, our spirits soar,
Ghostly heirlooms from days of yore.
Each faith-filled gaze, a treasure bound,
In holy echoes, truths are found.

Through the years, the candles burn,
In sacred silence, we discern.
In every hymn, a story lies,
Of love that dwells beyond the skies.

The altar holds our hopes and fears,
A tapestry woven from our tears.
In every hand that grips the stone,
The holy heritage we own.

As shadows linger near the dawn,
In every heart, your light is drawn.
The gathered souls, united plea,
In ghostly heirlooms, we are free.

Let us remember, let us keep,
The sacred trust, the faith so deep.
In worship's arms, we find our way,
With every night, we welcome day.

The Silent Benediction of Goodbyes

In quiet reverie, we stand apart,
The silent benediction warms the heart.
With every farewell, a promise made,
In sacred trust, our fears will fade.

As shadows fall, we lift our gaze,
In parting whispers, love's sweet praise.
The threads of life, entwined and spun,
In every tear, we find the sun.

In every sigh, a blessing flows,
Through empty halls, the spirit grows.
Each goodbye holds a memory bright,
In holy echoes, lost to sight.

The journey calls, the road unfolds,
With every step, your grace upholds.
In silence shared, where hearts align,
We bow with faith, your love divine.

So let us go, yet never part,
In every farewell, a sacred heart.
The silent benediction we embrace,
A whispered prayer, your boundless grace.

The Spiritual Weight of Goodbye

In stillness, hearts entwined,
A sacred bond, now unconfined.
The echoes linger, softly speak,
Of love that graces the strong and weak.

We gather tears like pearls of light,
Each drop a prayer in the night.
When paths diverge, and souls take flight,
We send them forth, our spirits bright.

The weight of farewells, a gentle grace,
Holds memories eternal in time and space.
For every end is a new dawn's start,
A promise kept within the heart.

In shadows cast, our hopes align,
The threads of fate, so pure, divine.
Though distance blurs the hands we hold,
Our love transforms, a truth re-told.

With each farewell, we rise above,
The silent whispers, the stories of love.
In every ending, a blessing lies,
In every tear, the spirit flies.

In Praise of the Unheld

In quiet moments, truth resides,
Where unheld hands, the spirit guides.
Though touch eludes, the heart perceives,
A deeper bond, the soul believes.

For in silence, whispers grow,
In absence found, the love will flow.
The unseen ties that bind us tight,
Illuminate the darkest night.

In fleeting glances, worlds collide,
A realm beyond, where dreams abide.
Though bodies part, the essence stays,
In echoes soft of tender days.

We sing of love that knows no chains,
Of joy that flows through subtle pains.
Though unheld, our spirits dance,
In endless grace, a sacred chance.

With every breath, the air is filled,
With unspoken prayers, our hopes instilled.
We praise the bonds unseen and true,
In realms of faith, forever new.

Crescendo of Distant Echoes

In valleys deep, the whispers rise,
Like distant hymns that fill the skies.
Each echo carries a tale divine,
Where love and loss, in harmony, align.

Through time and space, our voices blend,
A sacred chorus, we shall send.
In every heartbeat, the truth resounds,
A symphony of grace, where hope abounds.

From shadows cast, the light breaks through,
In every dream, a promise true.
The distant echoes call us home,
In unity, we shall not roam.

The crescendo swells, our spirits soar,
In unity's embrace, we find the door.
To realms unseen, where love will meet,
In every sound, the heart's retreat.

So let the echoes dance with flair,
In gratitude, we rise, we share.
For every note, a prayer's ascent,
In sacred harmony, our souls content.

The Covenant of Forgotten Moments

In fleeting time, we weave the threads,
Creating bonds where memory spreads.
The moments lost, yet held so dear,
In quiet corners, the spirit's cheer.

A glance, a smile, a shared embrace,
Reside in shadows, a sacred space.
Though years may pass, they still remain,
The covenant forged through joy and pain.

For every heartbeat, a promise made,
In light and darkness, love will wade.
Forgotten moments now reclaimed,
In whispered prayers, our hearts untamed.

We gather fragments, the pieces whole,
The echoes of a singular soul.
In every sigh, our lives entwined,
A testament of love, divinely designed.

So let us cherish the simple threads,
In the tapestry where the spirit treads.
The covenant holds, a bond profound,
In the heart's embrace, we are unbound.

Pilgrimage of the Heart's Surrender

In the stillness of dawn's embrace,
Whispers of grace fill the air,
Each step a prayer, lost in time,
A journey led by love's stare.

Through mountains high and valleys low,
The heart bears its weight, yet soars,
In trials faced and burdens shared,
The sacred path forever endures.

With every breath, the spirit sings,
Echoes of faith in each beat,
In surrender lies the freedom sought,
The humble heart finds its retreat.

Hands raised to the endless sky,
Invoking peace, a silent plea,
In unity, our souls arise,
Bound together in harmony.

At journey's end, a flame ignites,
The light within begins to shine,
In the pilgrimage of hearts laid bare,
We find the love that is divine.

Celestial Remnants of Days Past

In twilight's glow, reminiscence brews,
Echoes of laughter, shadows of pain,
Stars bear witness to stories untold,
Celestial remnants that still remain.

Each moment a thread in the fabric of grace,
Woven together in sacred design,
A tapestry rich with the colors of life,
Reflecting the joys that were once aligned.

With hearts open wide, we recall the light,
That guided us through the darkest of nights,
Each lesson learned, a blessing bestowed,
In the fabric of time, we find our rights.

The moon sings softly to all who will hear,
Of paths once traveled, of dreams chased in flight,
In celestial realms, we dwell evermore,
With remnants of love, both gentle and bright.

As seasons shift and the years ebb away,
Memories linger, a sweet, tender balm,
In the silence of night, we embrace the past,
Holding close to the remnants that bring us calm.

Spiritual Echoes of What Was

In the hush of twilight, whispers abound,
Spiritual echoes of what once was here,
Resonating softly in heart and in mind,
A symphony sweet, both distant and near.

Footsteps of those who have walked this path,
Leave traces of wisdom in footprints of light,
Their voices entwined in the fabric of time,
Guide seekers along through the depths of the night.

In shadows that linger, the spirit takes flight,
Recalling the dreams, the desires that glowed,
A tapestry woven with threads of the past,
In the heart of the seeker, each lineage flowed.

In the dance of existence, we raise our gaze high,
For in every heartbeat, the truth is revealed,
In echoes of spirit, our stories live on,
A connection eternal, forever sealed.

So we walk on this journey, our eyes ever wide,
With love as our compass, through time we will soar,
In the echoes of ages, we'll find unity,
In the spiritual tapestry, we are evermore.

The Sacred Dust of Our Steps

In the earth beneath, where the spirit does dwell,
Lies sacred dust of the paths we have tread,
Each step a communion, each moment a gift,
The journey of souls, in silence, we spread.

Through the fields of faith and the valleys of doubt,
We wander in search of the truth that we seek,
In the harmony found, our hearts intertwine,
In the sacred dust, our souls gently speak.

With wisdom of ages, our footprints remain,
In the soft morning light, they glimmer and shine,
A testament written in the sands of time,
Together we walk, with purpose divine.

The sacred dust tells tales of the brave,
Of dreams that were nurtured, of hearts set free,
For in each grain lies the essence of love,
Through every journey, we find harmony.

As we traverse this world, our spirits unite,
With reverence, we honor the steps we have made,
In the sacred dust, we find all we need,
A legacy lived, with grace and with faith.

The Seed of Yesterday's Promise

In the garden of time, hope does grow,
Each seed a whisper, a tale of tomorrow.
From the soil of faith, roots entwine,
Nurtured by grace, a sacred design.

Beneath the sun's gaze, dreams take flight,
Carried by winds into the night.
A promise cradled in every bloom,
Resurrected dreams banish the gloom.

Fertile ground waits for hearts to sow,
The harvest of faith, a wondrous show.
In the embrace of love, we shall find,
The essence of peace, transcending time.

With hands uplifted, we seek the light,
Guided by stars that pierce the night.
Each step forward, a dance with fate,
In the seed of promise, we celebrate.

As shadows deepen, our spirits rise,
In the arms of grace, we realize.
The journey unfolds, a sacred quest,
In every heartbeat, love is expressed.

Ascension of Forsaken Dreams

In silence they linger, the dreams of old,
Whispers of courage, stories untold.
Like feathers of angels, they soar on high,
Casting shadows of hope across the sky.

With each rising sun, new chances begin,
The spirit ignites, breaking the skin.
Forsaken no longer, ignited with fire,
They dance with the stars, lifting hearts higher.

A symphony composed of light and sound,
In the stillness of night, their echoes abound.
Through valleys of sorrow, they find their way,
In the spirit of love, they long to stay.

From ashes of doubt, a phoenix will rise,
Transforming the pain into brilliant skies.
A brave resurrection, they whisper and cry,
The ascension of dreams, forever we fly.

In the tapestry woven with threads of grace,
Each dream a stitch, a sacred place.
With hearts entwined, in unity gleam,
Embracing the light, we honor the dream.

Chronicles of Abandoned Sanctity

In shadows where whispers of silence dwell,
Old sanctuaries breathe a forgotten spell.
Once filled with laughter, now echoes remain,
Chronicles etched in the remnants of pain.

Sacred the ground where the faithful stood,
Tales of devotion, the pulse of the wood.
Time weaves a tapestry thick with the tears,
Of hopes that were born, of long-vanished years.

The fragrance of incense still dances in air,
Lingering memories held deep in prayer.
With each gentle breeze, the spirits roam free,
Guardians of faith, the past's decree.

In the heart of the silent, the truth lays bare,
A call for redemption, a promise to care.
Amidst the ruins, a light starts to break,
Awakening souls for the old sanctuary's sake.

As time moves forward, we carry the flame,
Honoring those who once whispered His name.
In chronicles woven with strands of grace,
We rekindle the sacred, embrace the space.

Reverent Paths of Yesteryear

The paths once tread by the ancients' might,
Whispering stories beneath the moonlight.
In reverent steps, where shadows recede,
We walk hand in hand, where hearts still bleed.

Each footfall echoes, a song of the past,
Lessons in love, memories to last.
Through meadows of sorrow, we find the thread,
That binds us to wisdom, where angels tread.

In the stillness of twilight, we gather our dreams,
Casting our burdens in shimmering beams.
With eyes of reflection, we honor the years,
Filled with laughter, and also with tears.

From the burdens we carry, light shall emerge,
Where faith meets our spirit, destinies surge.
In every heartbeat, in every sigh,
Reverent paths guide us, as we rise to the sky.

With hearts open wide, we embrace what's near,
Legacies cherished, a journey sincere.
In reverent paths, our souls intertwine,
A tapestry woven through space and time.

Footsteps on Sacred Paths

In gentle whispers, spirits tread,
A journey marked by faith instead.
With every step, the heart does soar,
In hallowed ground, we seek for more.

Beneath the stars, we raise our hands,
In unity, across all lands.
The light of truth, a guiding flame,
In sacred paths, we seek His name.

Through trials faced, our spirits grow,
In darkest nights, the blessings flow.
Each footprint left, a tale we share,
In love and grace, His presence there.

With open hearts, we sing His praise,
In every breath, His love displays.
The sacred paths that intertwine,
In every soul, a light divine.

As angels watch from skies above,
We walk as one, in perfect Love.
With footsteps light, and voices clear,
We journey forth, without a fear.

Beyond the Veil of Our Departures

When night descends and shadows creep,
We find the strength in silence deep.
Beyond the veil where we must part,
A bond remains in every heart.

In whispered prayers, our hopes arise,
As we seek truth in the skies.
A journey onward, yet still near,
In every tear, the love is clear.

Through memories held, we find our way,
As stars align, they softly sway.
The light of those who've gone before,
Reminds us how to love and soar.

Beyond the veil, our souls entwine,
In cosmic dance, forever shine.
With every heartbeat, they are here,
In every breath, we draw them near.

So let us walk on paths of grace,
With courage strong, we'll find our place.
In love's embrace, we shall remain,
Connected still, despite the pain.

The Graceful Heaviness of Memories

In gentle folds of shadowed nights,
We hold the past in soft twilight.
The weight of memories we caress,
A tapestry of love's excess.

Each moment etched, a sacred art,
In every breath, the echoes start.
Through laughter shared and sorrows deep,
In timeless bonds, our spirits leap.

The grace of time, it flows like streams,
In whispered prayers and fleeting dreams.
A heart that mourns, yet still holds light,
In sacred dances that take flight.

Through joy and pain, we find our way,
In every sunset, a new day.
The memories linger, soft but bright,
Guiding us through the shadowed night.

With every tear, a lesson learned,
In every flame, a passion burned.
The grace we find in shadows cast,
Becomes our strength, a love steadfast.

Silent Sacred Spaces in Our Souls

Within the silence, whispers dwell,
In sacred spaces where we quell.
The heart retreats to find its song,
In stillness deep, we all belong.

Amidst the chaos of the day,
We seek the truth; we long to pray.
In quietude, our spirits rise,
In hallowed light, we touch the skies.

The sacred hush within us grows,
A gentle river that freely flows.
In these still waters, grace does bloom,
Illumined paths dispel the gloom.

As daily burdens start to fade,
In silence, we embrace the shade.
The sacred spaces deep inside,
Awaken hope and love as guides.

Together here, as one we stand,
In silent prayer, we touch His hand.
In these moments, hearts align,
In sacred spaces, love divine.

Celestial Dust Upon Forgotten Paths

Upon the trails where shadows tread,
A whisper of grace, the heart is led.
In silent prayer, the soul takes flight,
With celestial dust, gleaming bright.

Each step, a prayer, a sacred quest,
In the echoes of faith, the weary rest.
The stars above, like candles glow,
Guiding the spirits where love can flow.

In the night, beneath the veil,
A presence felt, in soft exhale.
With every dawn, a promise new,
A path reborn, beneath the blue.

The moonlight dances on weary ground,
Where lost and found are closely bound.
Celestial dust upon our feet,
Revealing truths that make us complete.

And as the journey unfolds in grace,
We find our home, our sacred space.
The heart remembers, the spirit yearns,
In every lesson, the soul returns.

Traces of Light Beneath the Stars

In the quiet night, where shadows play,
Traces of light guide our way.
With every star, a tale untold,
Woven in silence, pure and bold.

Beneath the vastness, whispers soar,
In every heartbeat, forevermore.
The cosmos sings in harmony,
Together we walk, in unity.

Lost in wonder, in the soft embrace,
The light reveals the sacred space.
With faith as our lantern, bright and true,
We journey onward, me and you.

In falling stardust, dreams ignite,
Moments of grace, a heavenly light.
We gather hope like morning dew,
In traces of light, our spirits renew.

Every glance skyward helps us see,
The threads of fate, the tapestry.
In every sparkle, love's design,
Traces of light, forever divine.

Moments Captured in Heavenly Stillness

In the hush of dawn, where time stands still,
Moments captured, hearts we fill.
With breath of angels, softly we sigh,
In heavenly stillness, the spirits fly.

Each pause a prayer, each blink a gift,
In sacred stillness, the soul will lift.
The echoes of grace in the morning light,
A reminder of love, burning bright.

In stillness found, a wisdom deep,
Where shadows dance and secrets sleep.
With every heartbeat, a promise shared,
In moments precious, we are prepared.

As nature whispers, the world aligns,
In quietude, the heart entwines.
The sacred rhythm, a sweet refrain,
Moments captured, beyond the pain.

In these still chambers, peace abides,
Love's gentle presence, our hearts confide.
Together we rise, in the softest grace,
Moments captured, in love's embrace.

Pilgrims' Echoes in Sacred Time

In the steps of pilgrims, echoes ring,
A melody sweet, the heart takes wing.
Through valleys deep and mountains high,
In sacred time, we learn to fly.

With every journey, wisdom flows,
A path of faith, where grace bestows.
In unity we stand, hand in hand,
As pilgrims' echoes fill the land.

The ages whisper through trembling leaves,
In sacred stories, the heart believes.
From ancient lands to future dreams,
We walk in light, or so it seems.

With love as our compass, we seek the day,
To understand the sacred way.
Each echo lingers, a gentle call,
In sacred time, we rise, we fall.

As stars align in the evening sky,
We find our purpose, never shy.
Together we wander, in peace's embrace,
Pilgrims' echoes, a holy trace.

The journey unfolds, a tapestry spun,
In sacred time, we're all as one.
With every heartbeat, we share this rhyme,
In pilgrims' echoes, we find our climb.

Soulful Footprints on Sacred Earth

With each step upon the ground,
I leave my heart in silent prayer.
The soil bears witness to my quest,
And dares me to reflect and care.

The sun bathes me in golden light,
As shadows dance with morning dew.
I walk the path of ancient souls,
Their wisdom whispers, tried and true.

In every footprint, stories dwell,
A tapestry of love and pain.
I tread with reverence, so aware,
This sacred earth, my heart's refrain.

Mountains echo my humble call,
Their majesty aligns with grace.
In valleys deep, I find my peace,
In nature's arms, I find my place.

To wander on, my spirit high,
With open heart, I seek the light.
These soulful footprints guide my way,
Through day and night, towards the right.

Threads of Faith We Weave

In every heart, a thread of gold,
Woven tight with dreams and hope.
Through trials faced, our stories told,
We find the strength to rise and cope.

Each moment shared, a sacred bond,
Stitched with kindness, love, and care.
Together what we each respond,
Is woven in the very air.

From hand to hand, the fabric grows,
As souls unite in joy and strife.
In faith we find the path that glows,
Illuminating our shared life.

With every thread, a lesson learned,
In struggles pure, and laughter bright.
The tapestry of love is earned,
A testament to our shared fight.

So let us weave with open hearts,
The threads of faith that bind us tight.
For in this craft, each spirit starts,
To find the way, to soar in light.

Remnants in the Whispering Wind

The gentle breeze carries a song,
Of voices lost but never gone.
In nature's breath, their echoes strong,
Whispering truths we build upon.

The rustling leaves share tales of old,
Secrets of love that linger still.
Each gust a memory, pure and bold,
A call to nurture, heal, and fill.

Through quiet realms where shadows play,
We grasp at moments that remain.
The whispering wind leads the way,
To solace found in every pain.

In twilight's glow, I feel them near,
Each sigh aloft, a guiding hand.
As soft reminders draw me here,
To find the peace in this vast land.

So when the winds begin to sing,
I pause to honor dreams unfurled.
In every breath, a sacred ring,
Of loved ones lost in this wide world.

Pilgrimage of Our Hidden Loss

Upon this road, we carry grief,
A pilgrimage through silent night.
With each step, we seek relief,
Illuminating hidden light.

The burdens heavy on our backs,
In every heart, a tale untold.
Yet through the dark, our spirit cracks,
And finds the strength to be bold.

We walk with shadows by our side,
Through valleys deep and mountains high.
In every tear, a soul has cried,
In each soft whisper, spirits fly.

In sacred spaces, memories dwell,
Remnants of love that never fade.
As we share stories, hearts swell,
In loss, we find that we are made.

So let this journey not imprison,
But be the path to healing grace.
With every footfall, our vision
Turns sorrow's loss to sweet embrace.

Wounds of the Spirit's Journey

In the shadows of the soul's great night,
We heal the wounds with faith's soft light.
Each scar a tale that time has spun,
Echoes of battles lost and won.

Through valleys deep and mountains high,
We search for truth where spirits fly.
With every tear, a lesson learned,
In moments dark, our hearts are burned.

The path can twist, the road can bend,
But in the journey, we transcend.
Each step we take, a prayer in stride,
With love and courage as our guide.

Though weary souls may seek to rest,
In trials faced, we are divest.
For every wound that leaves us sore,
We find a light, and seek for more.

In the silence, spirits sing,
A melody of hope they bring.
Through every wound, the heart's embrace,
We learn to dance in endless grace.

Celestial Candles in the Void

In darkness deep, we light a flame,
Celestial candles call our name.
Their flicker whispers songs of grace,
Guiding us through the vastness of space.

Each star a promise, brightly cast,
A beacon shining from the past.
In solitude, we find our song,
In unity, we all belong.

Embers flicker in the silent night,
Reminders of our inner light.
Through shadows vast, our spirits soar,
Boundless in love forevermore.

Though the void around us may feel stark,
Each candle glimmers, igniting the spark.
Together we stand, strong and free,
A constellation of humanity.

With every breath, a prayer we share,
In every heart, a sacred care.
Celestial bonds that cannot break,
A hymn of love for the world's sake.

Hymn of the Lost Horizons

Beneath the arch of endless skies,
We seek the truth with earnest eyes.
The horizon whispers tales unseen,
Of journeys long and places serene.

In every dawn, a promise waits,
To open wide the heaven's gates.
Though lost we feel, we still aspire,
For in our hearts, we hold the fire.

Each step away from comfort's reach,
Brings wisdom only pain can teach.
The horizon calls with sweet refrain,
Reminding us of joy in pain.

As shadows stretch and daylight fades,
The path reveals the light cascades.
In search of hope, we wander far,
Our spirits rise, like distant star.

In unity, our voices blend,
An anthem sweet that has no end.
The hymn of lost horizons sung,
A testament to hearts once young.

Treasures Buried in Silence

In silence deep, treasures lie,
Whispers soft that never die.
Each thought a gem, each dream a pearl,
In quiet hearts, the secrets whirl.

We sift through time, through hopes and fears,
Uncovering truths beneath the tears.
In stillness, wisdom softly speaks,
A gentle guide for all our seeks.

While voices fade, the soul remains,
In hushed embrace, love never wanes.
On pathways paved in silent grace,
We find our strength through every space.

For buried treasures may be small,
Yet in their worth, they hold us all.
In heartfelt whispers, life unfolds,
A tapestry of stories told.

Through silence, we learn to find,
The deeper meanings intertwined.
With every breath, the treasures shine,
Eternal love, the divine design.

The Lost Pages of Our Story

In the quiet of the night, we seek,
Lost chapters stitched from silent dreams.
Echoes of the heart, they softly speak,
Whispers woven deep in sacred seams.

Each tear we shed, a sacred ink,
Writ upon the parchment of our fate.
In the shadows, truth begins to link,
Finding grace in love that will not wait.

With every dawn, a new page dressed,
In colors bright, our faith does bloom.
The stories told, in spirit blessed,
Illuminate our journey from the gloom.

Now gather, child, and hear the call,
In the tapestry of memory's embrace.
For every rise, there comes a fall,
Yet in these pages, we find our grace.

So write anew, the tale unfolds,
With every heartbeat, fresh and bold.
In every soul, a story gold,
The lost pages, at last, retold.

The Communion of What We Forget

In silence shared, our souls entwine,
Communion found in muted prayer.
The moments lost, yet so divine,
In gentle grace, a wisdom rare.

We gather shards of what we miss,
Each fragment brings a spark of light.
In shadows lost, we find our bliss,
As memories dance, both day and night.

Forgotten paths where echoes tread,
Through winding roads, our spirits soar.
In fleeting thoughts, the heart is fed,
The sacred bond forevermore.

Rekindle fires of faith's embrace,
In every heart, a spark ignites.
Together finding our own place,
In holy stillness, truth ignites.

So let us weave with threads of grace,
The tapestry of love's embrace.

Signs of the Departed Journey

In every star, a tale is cast,
A journey marked by heavens high.
We walk beneath the shadows past,
In every breath, the spirits sigh.

Through valleys deep, the silence speaks,
In rustling leaves, the voices call.
Awakening hearts, the truth it seeks,
As nature whispers, we hear it all.

Each path we take, a thread unspooled,
A map of lives we've left behind.
In every footstep, love is schooled,
Reminding us of the ties that bind.

In sacred moments, time stands still,
Embracing us with gentle hands.
Through every loss, we find the will,
To honor love where memory stands.

So heed the signs, let faith ignite,
For in the journey, we find the light.

Relics of Our Pilgrimage

With every step, a relic claimed,
On paths where faith and doubt align.
Each burden borne, though life is named,
In trials faced, our spirits shine.

The stones we gather mark our way,
Each tells a tale of love's embrace.
In sacred breath, we learn to lay
Our hearts and hope in heaven's grace.

The pilgrimage, a quest so pure,
With every mile, our souls refined.
In searching hearts, we find the cure,
Through trials faced, new strength we find.

Let each relic remind us still,
Of journeys walked with humble grace.
Through pain and joy, with steadfast will,
We find our home in every place.

So let our stories intertwine,
As relics precious, strong, and true.

Faithful Footprints in Celestial Sands

In the morning light we rise,
Seeking the path with open eyes.
Each step laid in sacred ground,
Faithful footprints, peace profound.

Guided by the stars above,
In whispers soft, we feel His love.
Through trials faced, we find our way,
In celestial sands, we humbly pray.

Every sorrow, every tear,
Transforms into a prayer sincere.
With every heartbeat, hope renews,
In the light, our hearts choose.

Among the shadows, joy ignites,
Faith's embrace through endless nights.
In every journey, grace endures,
Celestial sands, His love assures.

Together we walk, hand in hand,
In this unity, we firmly stand.
For in faith's journey, we shall find,
The sacred footprints intertwined.

Woven Blessings of Goodbye

When parting words are softly said,
In woven blessings, love is wed.
Each memory crafted, a soft thread,
In the tapestry of hearts we spread.

Though distance stretches far and wide,
In every heartbeat, love won't hide.
The bond we share is strong and true,
In woven blessings, I embrace you.

Through the tears and bittersweet sighs,
Each farewell whispered, never dies.
In every dawn, new hope will bloom,
Woven blessings dispel the gloom.

In cherished moments held so dear,
We find the strength to persevere.
With gratitude for each small joy,
In woven blessings, we find the ploy.

So here we stand, though paths diverge,
In faith we trust, love's constant surge.
With gentle hearts, we bid goodbye,
In woven blessings, we fly high.

Ribbons of Remembrance in Autumn's Breath

With every leaf that falls away,
Ribbons of memories softly sway.
In autumn's breath, we pause to see,
Past whispers rise, forever free.

The golden hues remind us all,
Of cherished moments, great and small.
In the crisp air, our hearts reflect,
Ribbons of remembrance, love's respect.

Each season brings a silent prayer,
In every breeze, your spirit's there.
Though time may pass and years will roam,
In ribbons of love, you are home.

As twilight paints the sky so bright,
We gather 'round in love's pure light.
In every heartbeat, you remain,
Ribbons of remembrance, joy and pain.

And when the stars twinkle and gleam,
We hold your essence in every dream.
In autumn's breath, we'll always strive,
Ribbons of remembrance will survive.

Relics of Love's Pilgrimage

In every step on this sacred trail,
Relics of love's journey prevail.
Through mountains high and valleys low,
In faith we walk, our spirits glow.

The stones we tread speak of the past,
In unity, our bonds are cast.
With every prayer, a story shared,
Relics of love, forever bared.

Through trials faced and victories won,
In every heart, a battle's spun.
Faith guides us as we seek the light,
Relics of love, banishing the night.

Hand in hand, our dreams align,
In love's embrace, our souls entwine.
Each whispered promise, a vow so grand,
Relics of love, like grains of sand.

And at the end of this journey wide,
We'll find each other, side by side.
In every heartbeat, love will sing,
Relics of love, our sacred offering.

Celestial Melodies of What Was

In whispers soft, the stars do sing,
Of bygone days and eternal spring.
Each note a prayer, each breath a song,
Reflecting love, where souls belong.

The moonlight drapes the earth in peace,
While shadows dance, and sorrows cease.
In memory's grip, our hearts unite,
Guided by faith, into the night.

The winds of change blew ever near,
And in their wake, we shed our fear.
For in each moment, grace abounds,
In every heartbeat, love resounds.

Through trials faced, we find our way,
In sacred light, our spirits stay.
Celestial whispers beckon bright,
Embracing us in the endless light.

So let us weave these melodies true,
With every breath, we start anew.
In harmony, we rise above,
To share the gift of boundless love.

Sacred Silent Reminders of Grace

In quiet hours, the spirit stirs,
With gentle grace, our hearts confer.
A sacred silence fills the air,
In sacred moments, we lay bare.

The dawn awakens, a gift divine,
In every ray, His love does shine.
The flowers bloom with fragrant grace,
Each petal whispers, "You're embraced."

Through trials faced, His hand we seek,
In whispered prayers, we find the meek.
For in the stillness, truth reveals,
The depth of love, that time heals.

So walk this path with courage strong,
In sacred trust, we all belong.
Each heartbeat echoes, "You are known,"
In every breath, we're never alone.

And when the night descends once more,
We rise in light, like waves ashore.
With sacred silence, we embrace,
The unyielding warmth of grace.

The Eternal Garden of Departure

In gardens lush, where shadows play,
We find the light that guides our way.
Each bloom a promise, each blade a prayer,
In nature's hand, we lay our care.

Beneath the boughs where spirits sing,
A soft caress, the love they bring.
In cycles of life, we ebb and flow,
With every ending, new seeds grow.

The whispers of leaves, a hymn of peace,
In the sacred hush, our worries cease.
Through every path, we walk in grace,
In every farewell, love finds its place.

With sunlit skies, the dawn will rise,
In every tear, God never lies.
For love transcends the earthly fight,
In the eternal garden, we cling to light.

So fear not change, embrace the flow,
In every heartbeat, let love grow.
For in this garden, life departs,
Yet blooms anew in faithful hearts.

Unseen Angels in Our Wake

With quiet wings, they hover near,
Unseen angels, banishing fear.
In every shadow, in every light,
Their presence whispers, "You are right."

Through trials faced and burdens bare,
They guide our steps with gentle care.
Each tear we shed, they catch with grace,
In moments shared, we find our place.

The softest sigh, a sign they send,
In darkest nights, their love will mend.
For in our hearts, their warmth resides,
A sacred bond that never divides.

With every heartbeat, they draw near,
In sacred love, we hold them dear.
Each whispered prayer, a bridge we build,
In faith and trust, our spirits thrilled.

So let us walk with courage bright,
With unseen angels, in the light.
For in our wake, they leave a trace,
A path of hope, a touch of grace.

Unfolding the Layers of Departed Grace

In shadows deep, we find the light,
A whispered prayer, a guiding sight.
Each layer shed, like autumn leaves,
In their fall, the spirit weaves.

From every loss, a lesson blooms,
In quiet nights, the heart attunes.
We rise again, as souls take flight,
In the arms of grace, we ignite.

Through trials faced, our trust renews,
In the stillness, we hear the muse.
What once was pain, becomes our song,
In unity, we all belong.

As stars emerge from twilight's veil,
Hope's gentle breath begins to sail.
In every tear, a story told,
Of love that dares to be consoled.

And in the dawn, a promise glows,
Each step we take, the spirit knows.
In the folds of time, we find our way,
A tapestry of souls at play.

In the Silence, We Remember

In silence deep, where echoes dwell,
The whispered thoughts of love do swell.
Amidst the noise, we pause to weave,
The cherished bonds that never leave.

As shadows dance in evening's glow,
We gather close, in hearts we know.
The memories shared, a sacred thread,
In every word, the love still spread.

Through reverie, we trace the lines,
Of laughter shared and intertwined.
In every heartbeat, softly beats,
The rhythm of our love that greets.

As stillness wraps its velvet cloak,
We speak in prayers, in breaths invoke.
For in the quiet, truth is found,
In the sacred space, love is profound.

In twilight's embrace, we honor those,
Whose spirits linger, gently prose.
In the silence, we remember well,
The bond unbroken, the stories swell.

The Divine Canvas of Letting Go

On canvas wide, the heart unveils,
The hues of joy, through trials and travails.
With every stroke, we find release,
In the art of love, we find our peace.

The colors bright, like morning light,
Touch every shadow, every plight.
In soft surrender, our spirits soar,
As we let go, we gain so much more.

Through every tear, a lesson drawn,
The beauty crafted at each dawn.
With brush in hand, we paint anew,
In the void, the spirit grew.

And when the storms of life may rage,
We find the strength upon this stage.
For in the chaos, there lies a song,
In the dance of letting go, we belong.

The masterpiece of every heart,
In shared embrace, we play our part.
With every sigh, we breathe the grace,
In divine letting go, we find our place.

Etchings of the Sacred in Our Hearts

In sacred space, where silence reigns,
Etchings deep, of love remains.
Carved in souls, the memories hold,
The stories whispered, soft and bold.

Each heartbeat serves, like ancient script,
Of paths we've walked, of bonds we've whipped.
In the tapestry of cherished years,
The sacred flows, through laughter and tears.

In every glance, a tale unfolds,
Of timeless truths, of hearts consoled.
In gentle touch, the spirit speaks,
In every silence, the love peaks.

The canvas wide, our lives entwined,
In every moment, grace defined.
Through joy and sorrow, we're set apart,
Etchings sacred, in every heart.

As we gather, our stories blend,
In the circle of love, there's no end.
In unity we rise, like stars that gleam,
Etchings of the sacred, in every dream.

Silent Tribute to Our Inner Grace

In stillness we gather, hearts align,
Breath of the spirit, a sacred sign.
We honor the silence, the light within,
A tribute unspoken, where love begins.

Each moment a whisper, a gentle call,
Echoes of mercy, we rise, we fall.
Hands lifted upward, souls entwined,
Finding our strength in the love combined.

Through trials we journey, hand in hand,
Guided by faith, we take our stand.
With every heartbeat, grace we find,
A silent devotion, forever kind.

The beauty of quiet, the peace we hold,
Stories of old, in warmth retold.
Through shadows and light, we walk the path,
In silent tribute, we find our wrath.

With hearts like lanterns, bright and true,
We shine the spirit, together anew.
A tapestry woven, in threads of grace,
In the quiet moments, we find our place.

The Rhythms of Absence and Presence

In the void of silence, prayers arise,
Whispers of longing, beneath the skies.
Each heartbeat echoes, a lost refrain,
In absence, we seek, our joy and pain.

Presence unfurling, like petals wide,
In every still moment, the spirit's guide.
The dance of the now, with shadows cast,
In rhythm and grace, we hold the past.

When absence is present, love's tender face,
We share in the journey, a sacred space.
Through valleys of doubt, our faith refined,
In the embrace of the void, peace we find.

With each step forward, we're not alone,
Every breath shared, a heavenly tone.
In the melody sweet, our souls entwine,
The rhythms of life, forever divine.

In the dance of shadows, we touch the light,
Emerging from darkness, our spirits ignite.
The cycles of absence, presence in tune,
In the heart's gentle pulse, the world is in bloom.

Feathered Whispers of the Divine

Softly they flutter, the feathers fall,
Messages borne on the wings of all.
Touching our spirits, they glide and soar,
Feathered whispers, forevermore.

In the hush of the night, they come alive,
Carrying dreams where our hopes thrive.
Guiding the lost, with love's embrace,
Feathered divinity, a sacred grace.

Each flutter a promise, a prayer in flight,
Illuminating pathways, shedding light.
The chorus of angels, in melodies sweet,
In feathered whispers, our souls meet.

Through trials and storms, we seek their guide,
In gentle caresses, their faith abide.
A bond woven strong, unseen yet clear,
Feathered whispers, our hearts draw near.

In the hush of the dawn, they softly sing,
Caring the stories that hope can bring.
With wings of solace, we find our way,
Feathered whispers of the divine sway.

Traces of Our Heart's Prayer

In the depths of longing, we kneel and plea,
Traces of prayer, like waves on the sea.
Each sigh a testament, each tear a part,
In the fabric of faith, we weave our heart.

With every shadow, our spirits rise,
Tracing the heavens, beyond the skies.
Hands clasped in unity, hope's bright spark,
Together we journey, igniting the dark.

In moments of stillness, the soul takes flight,
Finding the rhythm, the power of light.
Through struggles and triumphs, the path we share,
In traces of prayer, love's eternal care.

When silence speaks loud, our hearts align,
In the echoes of mercy, love divine.
Each breath a gift, a promise to keep,
In traces of prayer, the bond runs deep.

As seasons turn gently, we hold the grace,
Carried by faith, in love's embrace.
With open hearts, we rise and declare,
In the traces of hope, we find our prayer.

Milton Keynes UK
Ingram Content Group UK Ltd.
UKHW020039271124
451585UK00012B/946

9 789916 8977